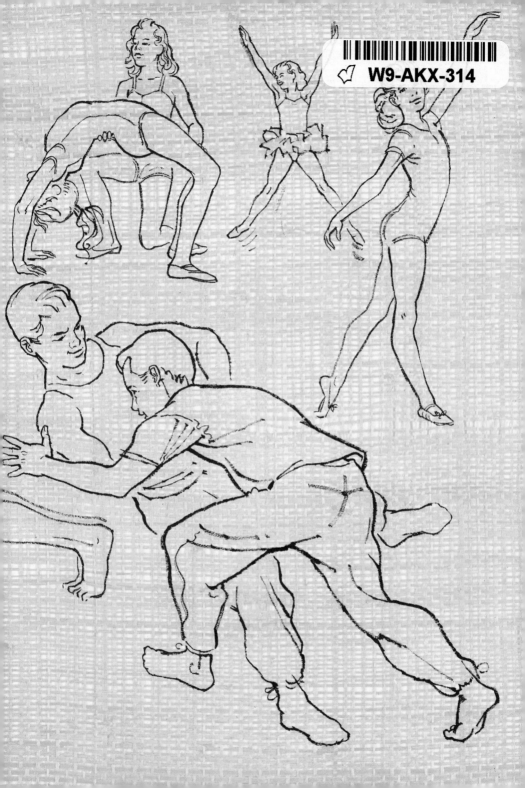

YOUR BODY

by HARRY SWARTZ, M.D.

illustrated by RALPH E. RICKETTS

WHITMAN PUBLISHING COMPANY

RACINE, WISCONSIN

Library of Congress Catalog Card Number: 62-14879

Copyright © 1962 by Whitman Publishing Company
All Rights Reserved

Printed in the U.S.A. by
Western Printing and Lithographing Company

CoNTENTS

1
YOU IN THE WORLD

PROBABLY THE MOST remarkable product of nature on this earth is the human being. And so since you are a human being, *you* are most remarkable. If you doubt this for even a moment just think of the many things you do during the course of a day.

In the morning you wake from sleep. Right away you begin to see, hear, feel, and become an active part of the world again. You rise from bed and go through all the complicated motions of washing and dressing. You take food, talk with your family. You walk, run, or ride to school. At school you work with your brain and hands. You study and learn. You play games. You ride a bike. Possibly you work at your hobbies.

And all along, while you are doing these things, your body is working automatically, on its own. Thoughts and feelings come and go. Your heart pumps blood through you, from your head to your toes. Your lungs fill and empty. Your stomach and intestines digest food.

What makes you more remarkable than cats, dogs, horses, and other animals? Can you guess? Here are some

9

of the answers many children have given to this question:

Because I can think and learn many things.

Because I can make things with my hands.

Because I can talk and make people understand what I want and think.

Because I walk upright on two legs.

If you put all of these together, and add a few more, you will come close to the right answer.

Some children have said, "The human body isn't so great. Look at some machines. There are electronic brains that do mathematical problems quicker than lightning. Jets fly high in the sky. Submarines go down deep into the oceans. Cranes lift loads of huge weight. Metal-turning machines can shape steel."

This is true, of course. But you must remember that man thought up these machines. He built them and made them work. They are of no use without man to run them. If man did not tend them, they would stop running.

And furthermore, your body grows. And some day you will have children of your own. Have you ever heard of a machine growing or having children?

Because you are so remarkable, we are going to look into your body. We are going to see of what and how it is made, and how it works.

2
INSIDE AND OUTSIDE... YOU

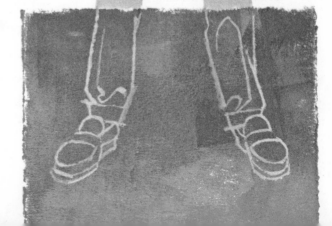

ALL LIVING THINGS are made of the same life material. It is called protoplasm. Protoplasm itself, however, is not a special material. It is made up of dozens of common substances—of salt, sugar, starch, fat, oils, alcohol, iron, copper, magnesium, and potassium. The only substance found in protoplasm and nowhere else in the world is protein. These substances make up 50 per cent of protoplasm. The rest is plain, ordinary water.

What makes protoplasm so special is simply the way these common things are put together, the way they are arranged. Think about bricks, steel girders, mortar, lumber, and electric wire lying about. Put them together, and depending on how you arrange them you can make houses, stores, garages, roads, and small bridges. That's

Here Are Some Amazing

1. GROWTH   **2. REPRODUCTION**   **3. SECRETION**   **4. DIGESTION**

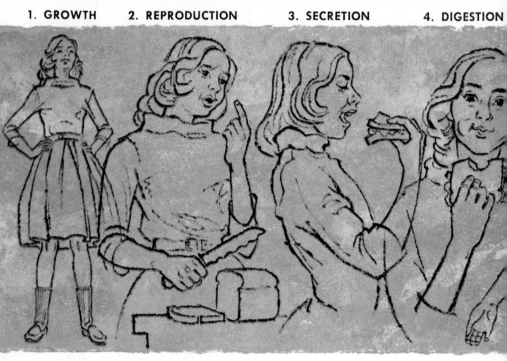

1. Growth takes place because of protoplasm.

2. When you cut yourself protoplasm forms more of itself to fill the gap. This healing is a kind of reproduction.

3. Saliva in your mouth and oil on your skin are the results of protoplasm. This is called secretion.

4. Food, broken down into liquid, makes its way into protoplasm. There it is used for energy and building.

the way protoplasm works, too, except that the different substances in protoplasm are constantly changing partners, moving about at different speeds. It is because of this constant movement that protoplasm is a remarkable

12

Things About PROTOPLASM

5. RESPIRATION   **6. MOTILITY**   **7. IRRITABILITY**

You breathe air into your lungs, and protoplasm uses the oxygen to release energy and get rid of carbon dioxide from broken-up food. Respiration takes place because of protoplasm.

Protoplasm is always moving, expanding and contracting. All of your movements are the result of protoplasm.

You pull your hand away from a flame or pinprick without even thinking about it. This is called irritability.

material—"alive" and producing the effects seen here.

All together the remarkable abilities of protoplasm shown on these pages make life possible. And only living things have *all* these unusual abilities.

13

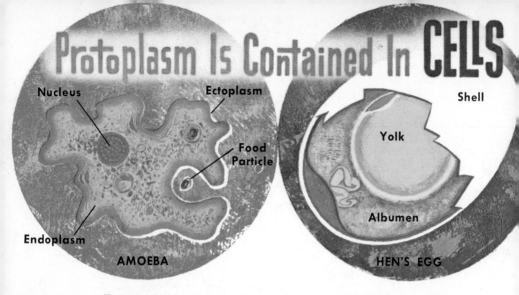

Nucleus

Ectoplasm

Shell

Yolk

Food Particle

Endoplasm

Albumen

AMOEBA

HEN'S EGG

Protoplasm occurs in units or cells. These differ in size. Some are so tiny, like the Amoeba, that they can be seen only through a microscope. The very largest cell is a bird's egg. Like the Amoeba, some creatures consist simply of one cell. Others, like you, are made up of several billion cells.

Cells are of different shapes. Generally, though, they are spherical, like a ball. Inside the sphere is a sticky liquid, the cytoplasm, meaning the protoplasm of the cell. Within the cytoplasm is a tiny ball of heavier material, the nucleus. Surrounding the cytoplasm is a thin, protective covering called the cell membrane. It is through this membrane that food and oxygen pass into the cytoplasm, and carbon dioxide and waste products pass out of it. If the cell membrane is badly injured, the cell will die.

Most of the daily jobs of living are done in the cyto-

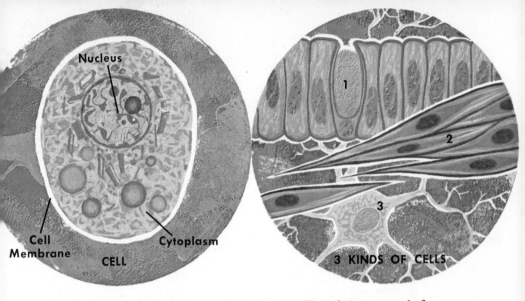

Nucleus

Cell
Membrane

Cytoplasm

CELL

1
2
3

3 KINDS OF CELLS

plasm. Here, digestion takes place. Food is stored for future use. Oxygen and carbon dioxide are exchanged.

In the nucleus lie all the materials the cell uses to reproduce itself.

Complicated creatures, like you, are made up of billions of cells. Certain of these cells have learned to do some particular job unusually well. But in the meantime, they have completely forgotten how to do certain other jobs. Such "educated" cells do their specialized job for the good of all the cells in your body. They, in turn, benefit by the jobs done by other specialist cells. Some of these specialized jobs are: carrying oxygen; breaking up food; manufacturing certain secretions. Because of the many types of specialists making up your body, you can do many more things and much more complicated ones than a single-celled creature like the Amoeba.

15

Groups Of Cells Form TISSUE

Cells that do the same kind of special work join together in great numbers to form tissue. There are six kinds of tissue in your body.

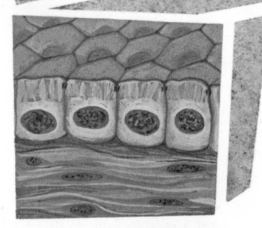

COVERING TISSUE

Covering tissue is the skin and lining of the mouth, throat, lungs, and other organs.

CONNECTIVE TISSUE

Connective tissue holds joints together, binds muscles in groups, and anchors organs in place.

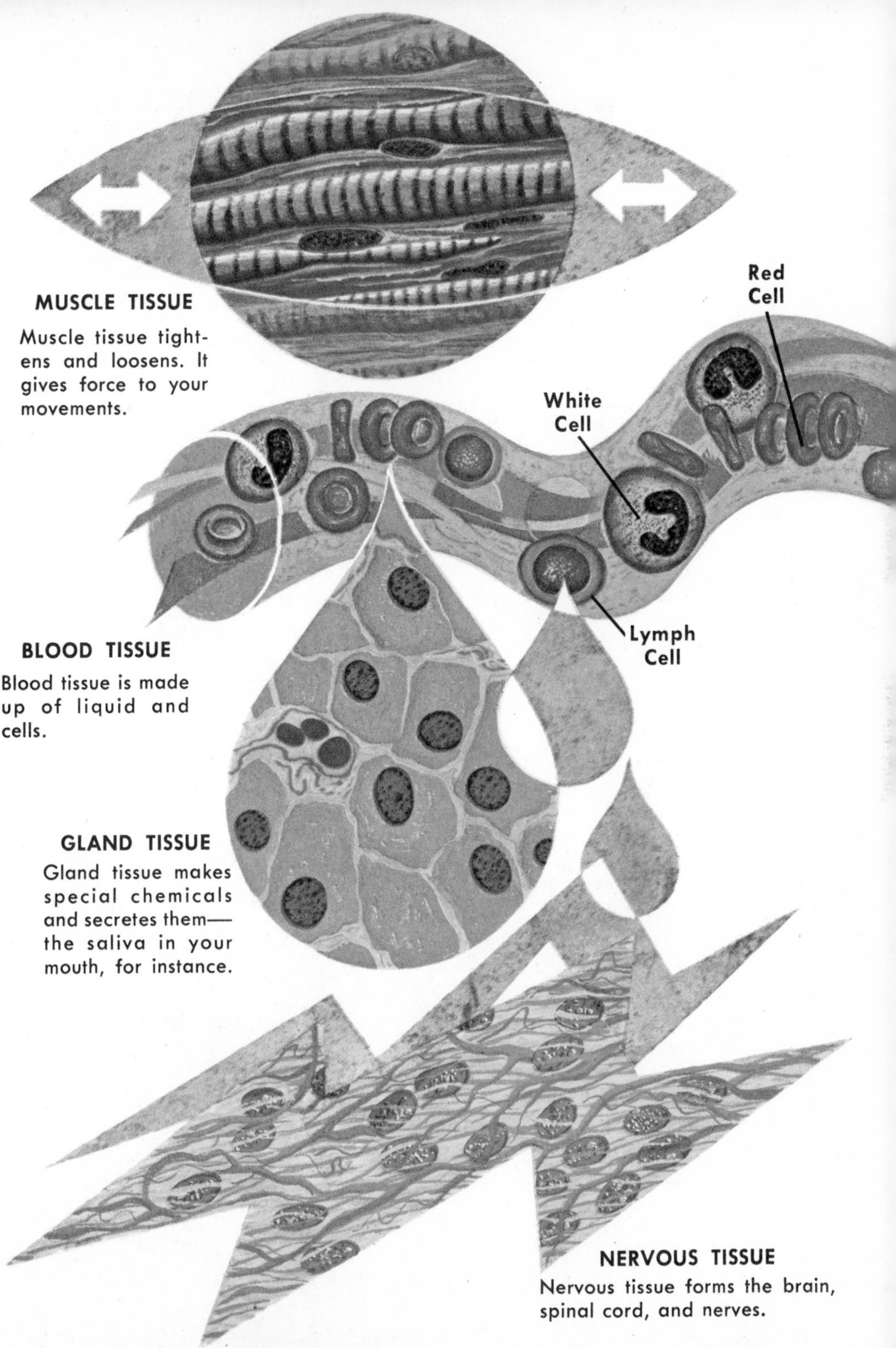

MUSCLE TISSUE

Muscle tissue tightens and loosens. It gives force to your movements.

Red Cell

White Cell

Lymph Cell

BLOOD TISSUE

Blood tissue is made up of liquid and cells.

GLAND TISSUE

Gland tissue makes special chemicals and secretes them— the saliva in your mouth, for instance.

NERVOUS TISSUE

Nervous tissue forms the brain, spinal cord, and nerves.

Groups Of Tissues Form ORGANS

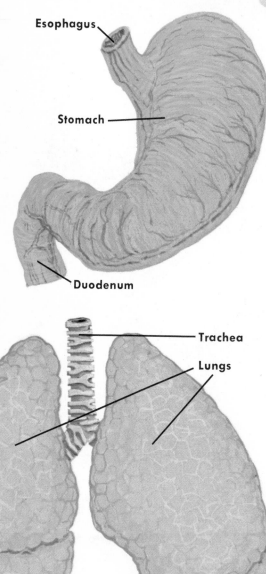

Esophagus

Stomach

Duodenum

Trachea

Lungs

Different tissues combine into organs to do a particular job. For example, the stomach is an organ made up of all six tissues. It is lined by covering tissue and has gland tissue that gives out certain juices. It has muscle tissue in its walls that churns food. Nerve tissue carries messages from and back to the stomach. Blood moves through its walls. Connective tissue anchors it in place and ties together the different tissues of which it is made. Other examples of organs are: heart, lungs, kidneys, liver, spleen, and brain.

18

Groups Of Organs Form SYSTEMS

Groups of different organs work together as systems to do complicated jobs. In all there are nine systems in your body: the lymphatic,

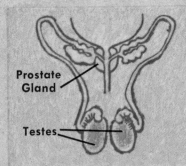

Prostate Gland

Testes

MALE REPRODUCTIVE SYSTEM

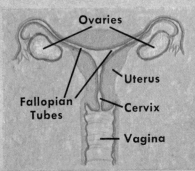

Ovaries

Uterus

Fallopian Tubes

Cervix

Vagina

FEMALE REPRODUCTIVE SYSTEM

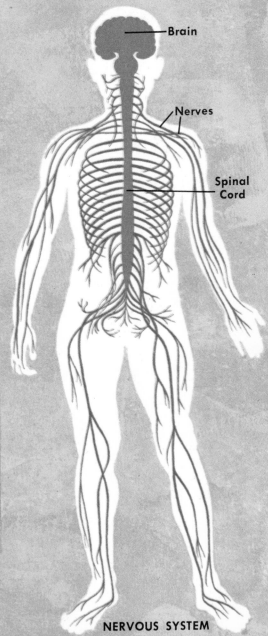

Brain

Nerves

Spinal Cord

NERVOUS SYSTEM

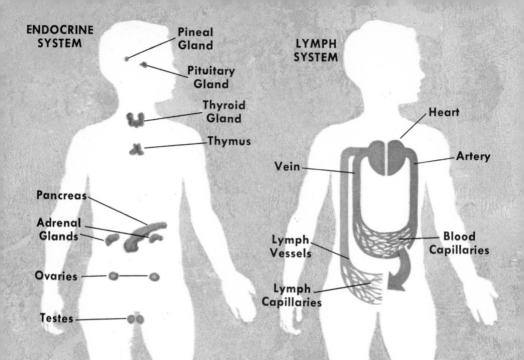

ENDOCRINE SYSTEM

Pineal Gland
Pituitary Gland
Thyroid Gland
Thymus
Pancreas
Adrenal Glands
Ovaries
Testes

LYMPH SYSTEM

Heart
Artery
Vein
Lymph Vessels
Blood Capillaries
Lymph Capillaries

The endocrine system is made up of glands that send their chemicals directly into the blood stream.

Lymph circulates through the body. It carries food and oxygen to the cells and carries away waste.

circulatory, nervous, endocrine, reproductive, skeletal, muscular, digestive, and respiratory.

So you see, cells form tissues, tissues form organs, and organs form systems. Nine systems make up your body but none can work alone. Each depends on the others.

3 TOUGH AND SOLID
Skin, The Body's Cover

YOUR SKIN COVERS your entire body. It protects you and does many special things necessary for life.

The outer part of the skin, the epidermis, is made up of several layers of flattened, dead cells. This forms a kind of armor for you. There are many tiny creases or folds in this armor that allow it to stretch easily when you move. On the finger tips the creases make a pattern which is different for each person. Your fingerprints are like your body's signature. No one else in the world has the very same prints.

Every day there is a great deal of rubbing of the epidermis. This knocks off the dead cells. New ones are formed by the underlayer of your skin, the dermis or true skin. However, if the rubbing or pressure is very great, the epidermis gets very thick and tough. Such a thickened place is called a callus. The callus protects the dermis against injury. The epidermis is so tough it prevents germs from getting into your body.

Under the epidermis, deep in the dermis, are hair

21

Hair

Epidermis

Dermis

CUTAWAY OF A FINGER

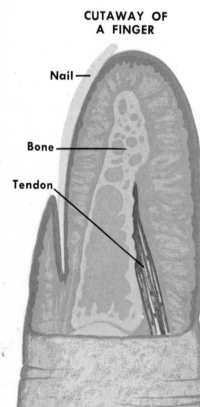

Nail —

Bone —

Tendon

Nails, made of dead cells, grow out of folds in the skin. As the live cells in the folds grow, they push dead cells to the outer edge.

roots. Each hair grows from its root through a shaft known as the hair follicle to reach the surface. Into each follicle a connected oil gland, a sebaceous gland, pours oil. The oil runs along the follicle and out onto the skin keeping it soft.

To each follicle is also attached a small muscle. Cold, fear, and anger tighten this muscle, pulling the hair straight and puckering the skin—"gooseflesh." This puckering makes the skin thicker and helps keep the heat in your body.

The skin helps keep the temperature of your body steady in another way. There are sweat glands in the dermis. These glands make a

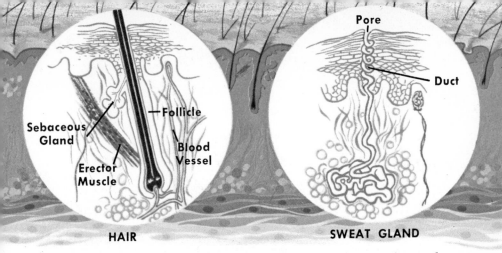

Sebaceous Gland

Erector Muscle

Follicle

Blood Vessel

HAIR

Pore

Duct

SWEAT GLAND

liquid and pour it into twisting tubes, or ducts, through which it reaches the surface of the skin. The openings of these ducts are called pores. Heat from sun, play, or work evaporates the sweat on the skin. This reduces the heat of the skin. Cold closes the pores, no sweat comes to the surface of the skin, and body heat is preserved.

The oil, sweat, and dead skin cells would cake and dry on your skin if you did not bathe. This is why bathing refreshes you and makes your skin feel so good.

The color of your skin depends on the amount of a dark pigment, melanin, made by special cells in the skin. The color of your parents' skin, sunlight, and special substances in your body called hormones determine how much melanin your skin will make.

There are also nerves in your skin. These help you feel pain. They let you know whether the things you touch are hot or cold, smooth or rough. They help keep you safe.

23

Bones, The Body's Solid Framework

The 206 bones in your body form the skeleton. This gives shape to your body. It also supports soft tissue, and protects your internal organs. Your bones are very tough and strong. They can carry heavier loads than brick and almost as much as iron.

In the bone center there is a soft, mushy tissue, the marrow. This makes the red and white cells for the blood.

The white, hard, outer case of the bones is the cortex. Tough as it is, it has thousands of tiny openings through which blood vessels carry food and oxygen to the marrow.

The cortex is made up mostly of two substances: calcium and phosphorous. These come from the food you eat. They are stored in the bones which give them off to your body as it needs them. Without these chemicals you could not stay alive.

The cortex is covered with a very thin, tough tissue called the periosteum that has many blood vessels and nerves. If the periosteum is seriously damaged, the bone will not grow properly or heal when broken.

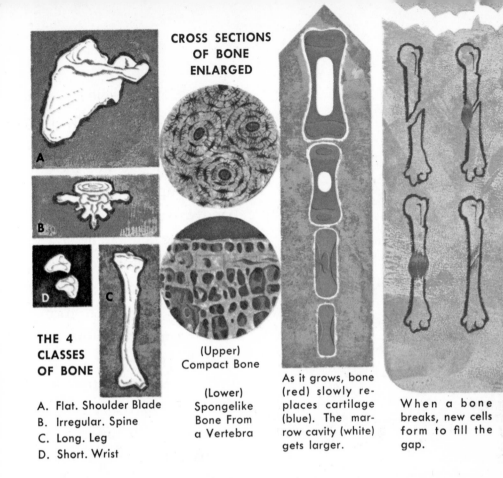

CROSS SECTIONS OF BONE ENLARGED

A

B

D

C

THE 4 CLASSES OF BONE

A. Flat. Shoulder Blade
B. Irregular. Spine
C. Long. Leg
D. Short. Wrist

(Upper) Compact Bone

(Lower) Spongelike Bone From a Vertebra

As it grows, bone (red) slowly replaces cartilage (blue). The marrow cavity (white) gets larger.

When a bone breaks, new cells form to fill the gap.

Most bones are hollow. They grow by getting bigger on the outside, while special cells eat away the inside. In this way, bones get larger and stronger but not much heavier.

When a bone breaks, new cells fill the gap. Gradually calcium is laid down among these cells forming a thick swelling called a callus. When the bone heals the swelling stops and the bone is stronger than ever.

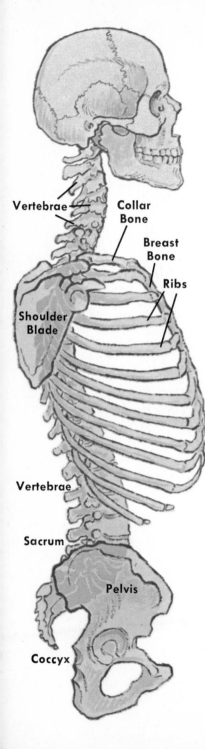

Vertebrae
Collar Bone
Breast Bone
Ribs
Shoulder Blade
Vertebrae
Sacrum
Pelvis
Coccyx

Your backbone or spine is the main support of your body. The spine is made up of thirty-three bones, the vertebrae. These fit one atop the other. In the grownup, the upper twenty-four can move one on the other while the lower nine cannot. The lowest four of these join to form one bone, the tail bone or coccyx. The five above the coccyx also join to form a single bone, the sacrum, in the small of the back.

The hollow centers of the vertebrae form a long narrow canal, the spinal canal. Through this runs the main nervous cable, the spinal cord.

Although teeth are part of the skeleton, they are not true bones. For one thing, they cannot heal themselves. For another, they are covered by the hardest tissue in the body, enamel. In the center of each tooth is a soft tissue, the pulp. This contains blood vessels and nerves. Between the enamel and pulp is a hard, elastic tissue, the dentine. Each tooth has roots that fix it in its socket in the jaw. The top surface of the tooth is called the crown.

You have two sets of teeth. The first or baby teeth number twenty in all. As you grow and your jaws become larger, these begin to fall out. The second set or permanent teeth begin to come in. These are tougher, and when they are all in they number thirty-two.

If you do not brush your teeth, the germs in your mouth attack the food bits caught between your teeth and form an acid. This may eat through the enamel and cause a cavity. When the cavity reaches the pulp, you will feel pain.

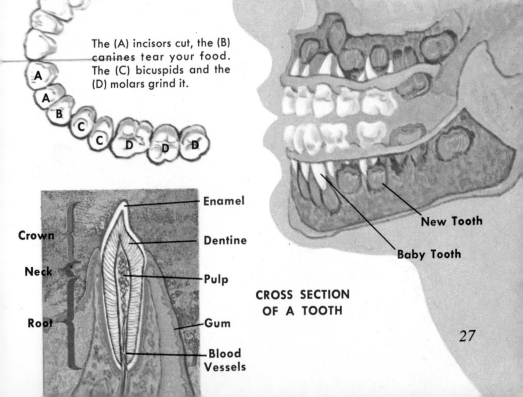

The (A) incisors cut, the (B) canines tear your food. The (C) bicuspids and the (D) molars grind it.

A
A
B
C
C D D D

Crown
Neck
Root

Enamel
Dentine
Pulp
Gum
Blood Vessels

New Tooth
Baby Tooth

CROSS SECTION
OF A TOOTH

27

Joints...

Your body can make thousands of movements because of the way the bone ends are connected with each other. Such connections are called joints.

In the skull, the flat bones fit closely together. Such joints are not movable. Other joints, as between the vertebrae in the spine, allow only limited movement. In the arms, hands, legs, and feet the joints are freely movable.

There are four main kinds of freely movable joints. Bend your fingers or knees. They work like door hinges.

HIP JOINT

Hip Bone

Cartilage

Muscle

Synovial Fluid

The bone-ends in a joint are covered with cartilage, which is smoother and softer than bone. Covering the cartilage and linking the joint is a tissue that makes a liquid called the synovial fluid, the oil of your joint.

Ligament

These are called hinge joints. Now turn the knob on a door. You see how your arm twists on the elbow? This is a pivot joint. Your thumb can make a wide circular motion, touching each finger. This is a saddle joint. Your hips and your shoulders have the most movable joints. You can swing your arm in a circle or move it in and out because it has a ball and socket joint.

Sheets of tough, fibrous, elastic tissue called ligaments bind the bone ends together. They keep the joints in position, but allow them to move.

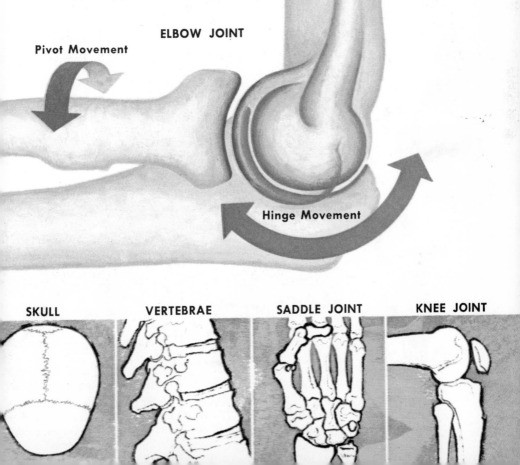

ELBOW JOINT

Pivot Movement

Hinge Movement

SKULL **VERTEBRAE** **SADDLE JOINT** **KNEE JOINT**

Muscles...

When these muscles shorten, the arm bends.

Filling out the shape of your body are large sheets and bands of muscle that lie between your skin and skeleton. There are more than six hundred, altogether. Most muscles go from one bone to another. When muscles shorten, bones move on their joints.

Groups of muscles work in pairs. One pulls one way, the other the opposite way. Between these two pulls you can control the degree of movement.

There are other muscles that do not move bones. The diaphragm, for example, helps the lungs inhale air.

When the muscles behind the knee shorten, the leg bends.

The muscles you can move at will

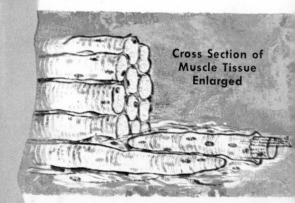

Cross Section of Muscle Tissue Enlarged

Some muscles are attached to tough cords called tendons, fastened to the bone. The two behind your knees are called the hamstrings. Another, above your heel, is the Achilles tendon.

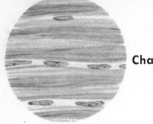

Chains of Tendon Cells
Enlarged

are called voluntary muscles. These are made up of long fibers that run in a sheath and are covered by tough membrane. Under the microscope, you can see that the fibers are made up of long, striped cells.

There are other muscles whose cells have no stripes and that cannot be moved at will. These are found in the organs and blood vessels of your body. They do their work automatically. They cause the movement of the stomach, intestine, and other organs. They are called smooth or involuntary muscles.

The more you use your muscles, the larger and tougher they become. They have tone. If you do not use them much, they become flabby, soft, and lose their strength. They lose tone. You can see why, then, it is important that you get plenty of exercise.

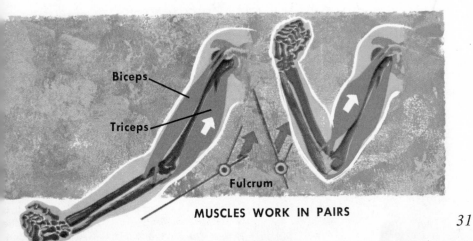

Biceps

Triceps

Fulcrum

MUSCLES WORK IN PAIRS

4 FUEL AND FLAME
The Digestive System

Y OUR BODY NEEDS FUEL in order to work. It also needs raw materials from which to build and repair itself. It gets both of these from the food you eat. This food, however, is mostly bulky and solid. In order to use this food, your body must break it down and make it liquid. Your cells then take from it the important parts they need. The rest you get rid of as waste.

It is your digestive system that does this job. This system is made up of the mouth, esophagus, stomach, intestines, and several glands—the salivary glands, liver, and pancreas.

The changing of food begins in your mouth. Your teeth cut, rip, crush, and grind the food while the tongue turns and mixes it. The saliva from the salivary glands wets it. A special substance in saliva, an enzyme called ptyalin, begins to break it down. This attacks the big starch bits, changing them to simpler sugars.

Finally, your tongue pushes the soft mass of food to the back of your mouth and into your throat. Muscles here force it down into the esophagus, a muscular tube

that goes straight down into the stomach.

After an hour or more, the stomach muscles squeeze the food paste through its lower narrow opening, the pylorus, and on into the small intestine.

The small intestine is a twenty-foot-long, narrow tube coiled and twisted to fit into the belly. Its muscular walls churn the food and move it along. The lining of this tube has millions of fine, hairlike projections, the villi. Through these the final broken-down liquid food passes into the blood and lymph.

The final breakdown of food takes place in the small intestine. Juices from the liver, pancreas, and

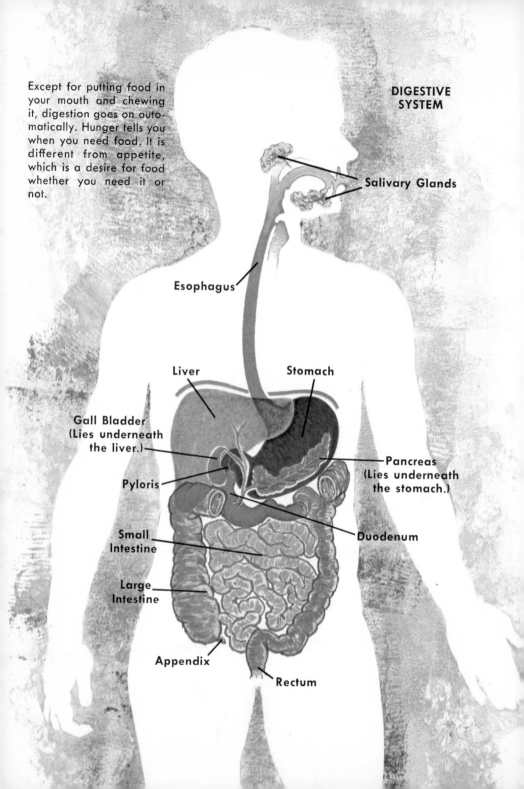

Except for putting food in your mouth and chewing it, digestion goes on automatically. Hunger tells you when you need food. It is different from appetite, which is a desire for food whether you need it or not.

DIGESTIVE SYSTEM

Salivary Glands

Esophagus

Liver

Stomach

Gall Bladder
(Lies underneath the liver.)

Pancreas
(Lies underneath the stomach.)

Pyloris

Small Intestine

Duodenum

Large Intestine

Appendix

Rectum

glands in the intestinal wall do this job. In these juices are numbers of other enzymes. Each attacks special parts of the food.

The large intestine is wider, heavier, and much shorter than the small intestine. It begins at the lower right side of the belly. Here a small wormlike tube, the appendix, hangs from it. The large intestine then goes up under the liver, across the belly to the left side, and then down where it becomes the rectum. The large intestine removes the liquid from the food mass, and the waste leaves the body through the rectum.

The broken-down food is led to the cells by the blood and lymph, as you will see later. For their work, the cells need sugar, such as glucose. This comes from carbohydrate food such as cereals, bread, cake, fruits, vegetables, syrup, and ordinary table sugar. From glucose the cells get energy when oxygen is present to "burn" it. When oxygen "burns" glucose, water and carbon dioxide result in addition to energy.

The cells may also burn fats for energy. But a good deal of it is stored away for future use. If you could not get food for a few days, your body would begin to use up its stores of fat. Fat comes from milk, butter, meat fat, oil, cheese, and nuts. It is stored mainly under the skin. Here it helps keep you warm.

In order to build and repair themselves, cells need protein. Digestion breaks protein down into amino acids. These are carried to the liver by the blood and broken down even more. They are then picked up by the cells and rebuilt into cell proteins. Protein of your food is found mostly in meat, fish, eggs, and milk products.

In addition to these foods, your body needs vitamins, minerals, and water in order to work properly. These all come from the food you eat. You can see, then, why it is important to eat the right kinds and amounts of food.

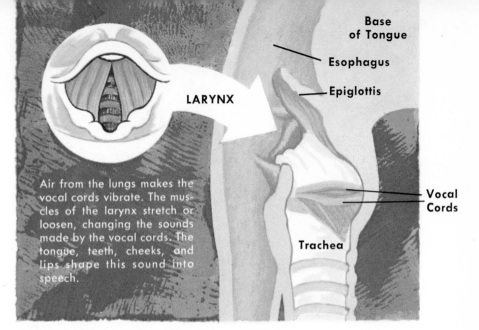

Base
of Tongue

Esophagus

Epiglottis

LARYNX

Vocal
Cords

Air from the lungs makes the vocal cords vibrate. The muscles of the larynx stretch or loosen, changing the sounds made by the vocal cords. The tongue, teeth, cheeks, and lips shape this sound into speech.

Trachea

The Respiratory System ......

Down your throat go food and air. Sometimes when you eat and talk at the same time the food may go down the "wrong pipe." Then you cough and choke and sputter until you get rid of it. What has happened? The food has started down the airway instead of the esophagus. In front of the esophagus and just a bit lower is the windpipe. On top of it and just below the tongue is the voice box or larynx, mainly made of cartilage. You can see and feel it as your Adam's apple. You notice that it goes up when you swallow? It rises against a small lid, the epiglottis, closing its entrance. Food cannot get into the larynx and must go down the esophagus.

37

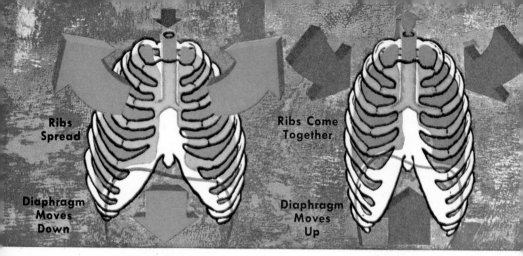

Ribs Spread

Ribs Come Together

Diaphragm Moves Down

Diaphragm Moves Up

Air Pulled In   **Air Pushed Out**

The air you breathe is cleaned, warmed, and moistened on its way through your nose. This job is done by coarse hairs, down-sweeping hairlike strands from the lining cells, mucus, and the many blood vessels in the lining tissue of your nose. The air then passes out the back of the nose, down the throat through the larynx, and into the windpipe or trachea.

The trachea is a tough muscular tube with many rings of cartilage in its wall. It is lined with tissue that has hairlike strands that sweep particles up and out of the lungs. Just below the neck, the trachea splits into two smaller tubes, the bronchi. One of the bronchi goes to the left lung, the other to the right lung.

The bronchi divide and redivide like the branches of a tree into a great many very small tubes. The smallest of these, the bronchioles, lead into air sacs that look like clusters of grapes. In the very thin walls of these sacs are

This is how you breathe. Muscles pull the ribs up and outward. The diaphragm contracts, causing the lungs to stretch. Air is sucked into them. Then the muscles relax. The ribs spring back and the diaphragm moves upward. This causes the lungs to squeeze together, pushing out the air.

Air Sacs

Artery

Vein

Veins trade carbon dioxide for oxygen in the lungs. Arteries carry oxygen through the body.

many tiny blood vessels. Here, the oxygen of the air passes into the blood, while at the same time carbon dioxide passes from the blood into the air sacs and out of the body.

The rush of air into the lungs is called inspiration. The rush of air out of the lungs is called expiration. Both in succession are called respiration. In grownups respiration takes place at the rate of sixteen to eighteen times a minute. A baby may breathe thirty to forty times a minute. When you exercise, run, play, work hard, get excited, or are sick, you breathe more quickly.

Breathing goes on automatically. You cannot hold your breath for very long before you are forced to breathe again. When you do not breathe, carbon dioxide gathers in your blood and is carried to a certain part of the brain. From the brain a strong command is sent out to your breathing muscles. This makes you breathe.

39

5 SUPPLY AND TRANSPORT

To carry oxygen and broken-down food to billions of cells in your body, your blood travels through a complicated network of tubes, the blood vessels. These reach into every part of your body.

Pumped out of the heart, your blood moves into the great blood vessels called arteries. Near the heart, these are about the size of a garden hose. Muscle and elastic tissue in their walls add force to the movement of the blood. As they go on from the heart, the arteries divide and redivide into many smaller ones. The finest and smallest are the capillaries through which the blood must move slowly. The walls of the capillaries are very thin. Through these thin walls the blood is able to give up its oxygen and food and pick up the cells' waste matter and carbon dioxide.

Your blood continues through the capillaries which begin to unite forming larger and fewer vessels, the veins. These lead back to the heart. The blue lines on your hands, arms, and neck are veins. In front of and just above the middle of your ears, your fingertip can feel the beat of an artery.

The Circulatory System

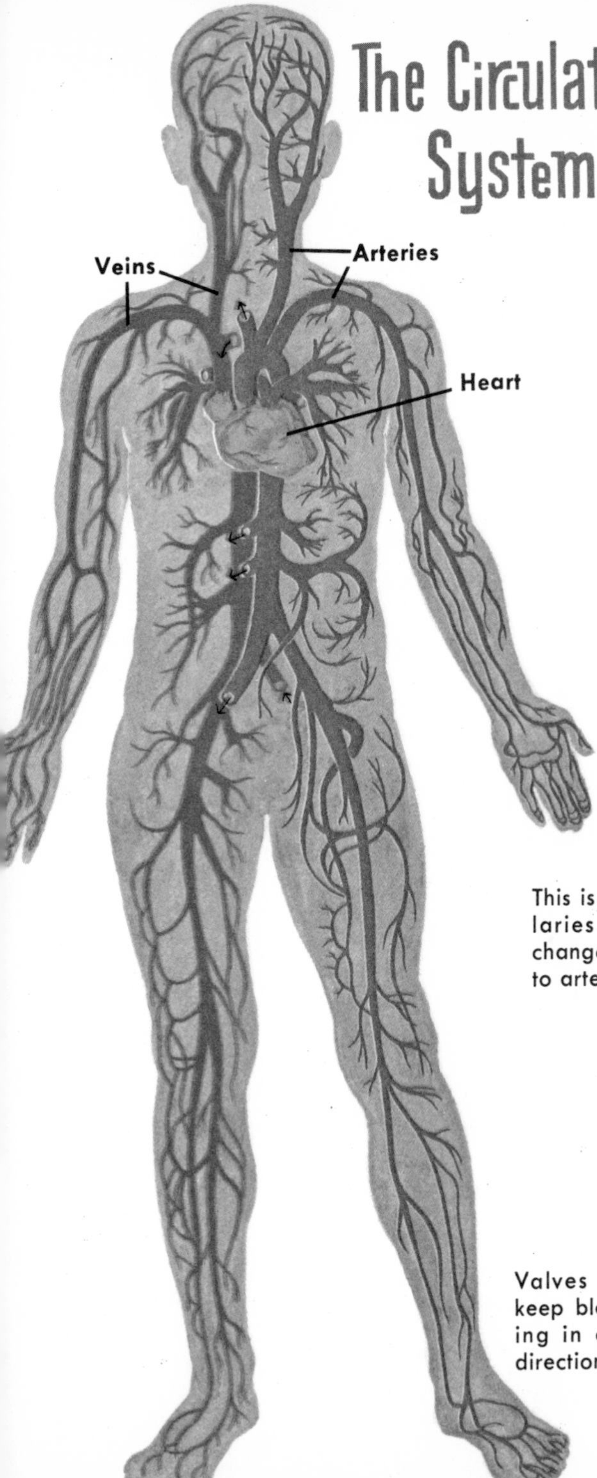

Veins

Arteries

Heart

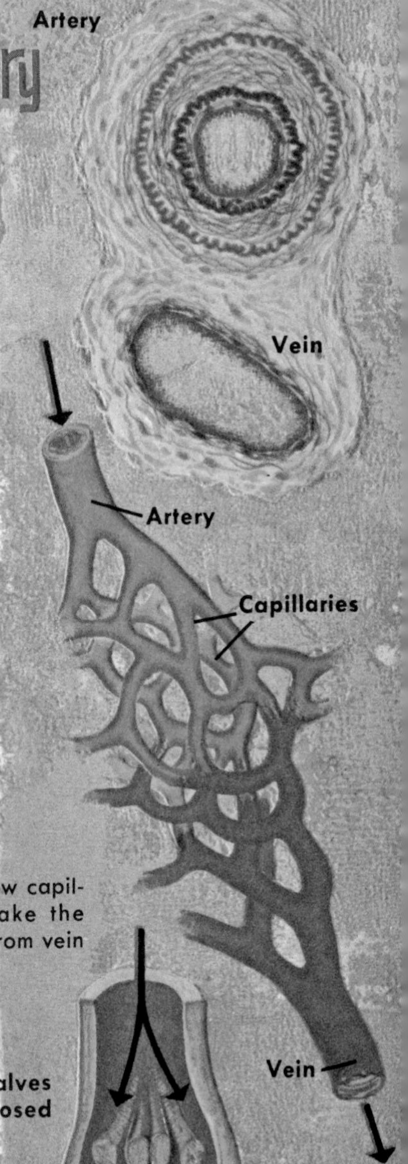

Artery

Vein

Artery

Capillaries

This is how capil-
laries make the
change from vein
to artery.

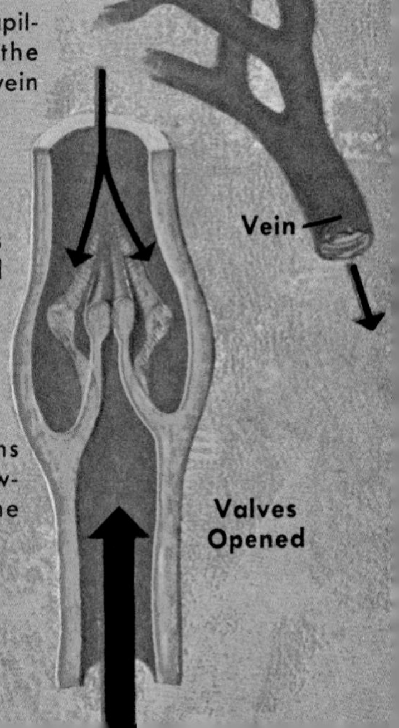

Valves
Closed

Vein

Valves in veins
keep blood flow-
ing in only one
direction.

Valves
Opened

The color of your blood is due to hemoglobin, a protein with iron in it. Blood turns bright red upon picking up oxygen in the lungs and is this color in the arteries. When blood gives up oxygen it becomes dark the way it is in the veins.

The veins are weaker and have thinner walls than the arteries. In them are small valves that keep the blood moving toward the heart. When an artery is cut, bright red blood comes in spurts. When a vein is cut, dark red blood flows out evenly. From this you can guess that blood pressure is greater in the arteries than in the veins.

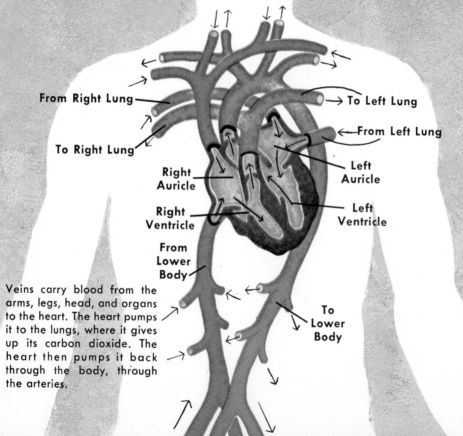

From Right Lung

To Left Lung

From Left Lung

To Right Lung

Right Auricle

Left Auricle

Right Ventricle

Left Ventricle

From Lower Body

To Lower Body

Veins carry blood from the arms, legs, head, and organs to the heart. The heart pumps it to the lungs, where it gives up its carbon dioxide. The heart then pumps it back through the body, through the arteries.

The Heart...

Your heart is a tough muscular pump about the size of your fist. It works day and night throughout your life without stopping. It is made up of a right and left half, completely separate from one another. Each of these halves is a pump. Each half has two chambers, one atop the other with a passage between containing a valve. The valve keeps the blood from flowing backward, making it move on. The upper chambers are smaller and weaker than the lower ones and are known as the auricles. The lower more powerful chambers are the ventricles.

The big veins bring the blood to the right auricle. With a little squeeze the right auricle passes it into the right ventricle. This begins to squeeze down and the valve closes preventing the blood from going back into the auricle. The blood is pumped into a large artery where another valve closes, preventing it from getting back into the ventricle. This artery leads the blood into the lungs. There it picks up oxygen and gives up carbon dioxide. The lung veins join into a number of larger ones and lead the bright red blood into the left auricle. From the left auricle it is forced into the left ventricle. From here it is pumped into the large arteries that lead the blood throughout the body to the capillaries, then the veins, and back to the right auricle.

The LUB DUB . . . LUB DUB you hear
through a stethoscope is the sound
of your heart valves closing.

White Blood Cells

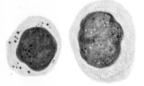

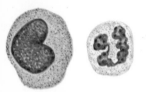

Red Blood Cells

Red blood cells carry oxygen to the body. White cells are defense soldiers. They attack germs and other impurities that get into the blood. There are about five hundred times as many red cells as white.

Blood and Lymph

Although blood looks red, the liquid part, the plasma or lymph, is straw colored and clear. Floating in this are disc-shaped red cells and white cells almost the same color as the liquid. These may be round or have irregular shapes.

The plasma leaves the capillaries through their walls and bathes the body cells. Here it makes the exchange of food and oxygen for waste and carbon dioxide. It also carries antibodies that protect you against infection. The plasma then goes back into the capillaries or into tiny lymph vessels that are found in great numbers throughout your body. These unite to form larger vessels that finally empty into veins. In this way the plasma returns to the blood. When plasma is in the lymph vessels it is called lymph.

The broken-down fat from food passes through the villi in the intestines and right into the lymph vessels. The glucose and amino acids go into the capillaries. Although the blood carries the food and oxygen supply to various parts of your body, it is the lymph

CIRCULATION OF THE LYMPH

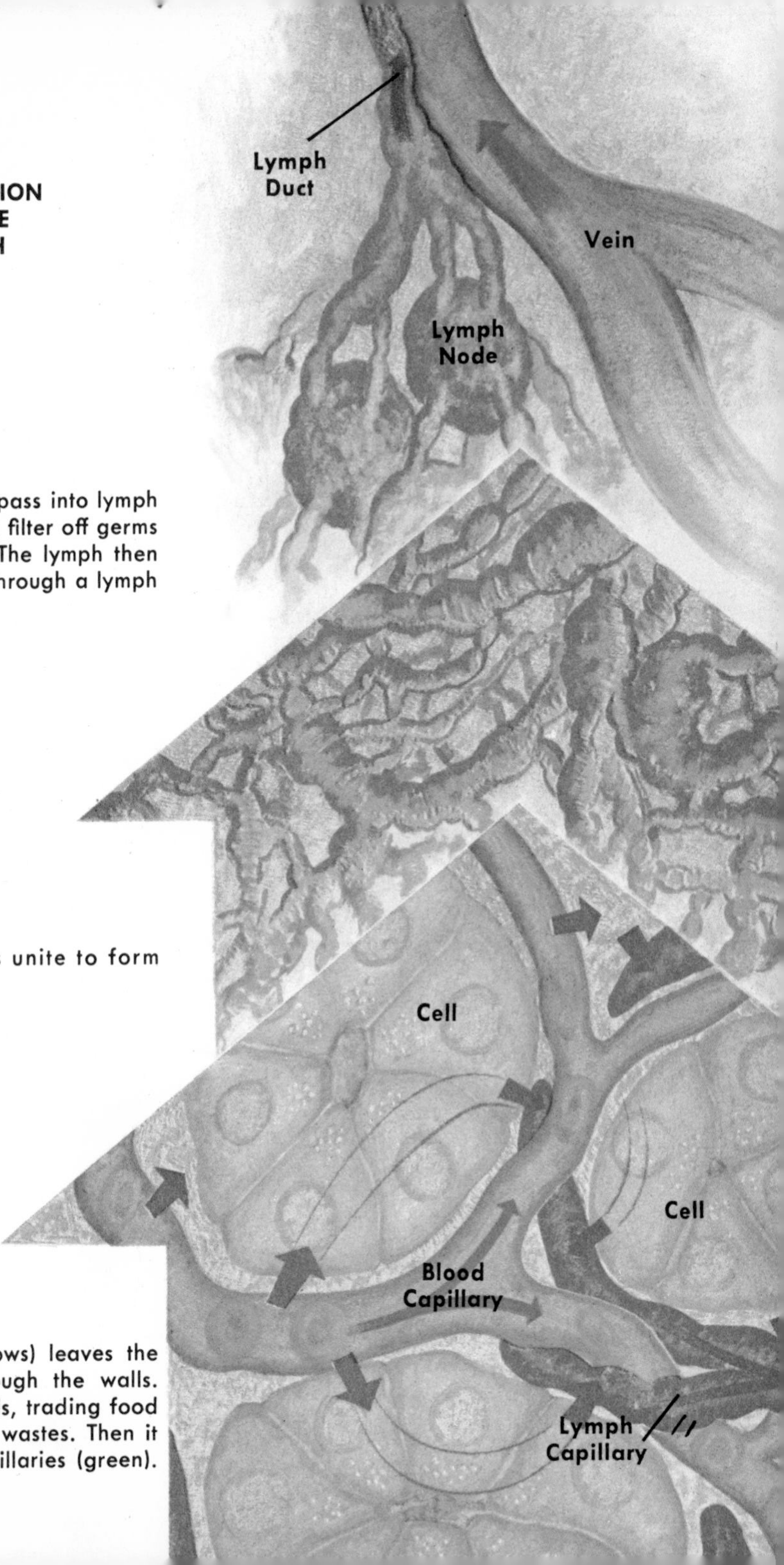

Lymph Duct

Vein

Lymph Node

C

C. The lymph vessels pass into lymph nodes or glands which filter off germs and other impurities. The lymph then passes into the veins through a lymph duct.

B

B. Lymph capillaries unite to form larger lymph vessels.

Cell

Cell

A

Blood Capillary

Lymph Capillary

A. Lymph (green arrows) leaves the blood capillaries through the walls. It bathes the body cells, trading food and oxygen for body wastes. Then it passes into lymph capillaries (green).

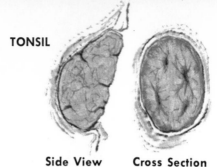

TONSIL

Side View   Cross Section

Tonsils and adenoids are examples of lymph glands. Smaller glands are found in many parts of the body.

and plasma that shuttle it to the cells.

The millions of lymph vessels pass through lymph nodes or glands on the way back to the veins. These filter germs and other impurities from the lymph.

Lymph, lymph vessels, and lymph glands are part of the lymphatic system. So is the spleen. This is a fist-sized organ in the upper left part of the belly under the diaphragm. It is made up of bunches of white blood cells with spaces between them through which the blood flows. The spleen does many jobs. It manufactures white cells. It acts as the graveyard for worn-out red cells. And it stores blood for emergencies.

THE SPLEEN

This spongelike organ is the largest lymph organ in the body.

The Liver...

The liver is the largest, heaviest, and one of the most important organs in your body. It lies just under the diaphragm in the upper right part of the belly.

The liver does many vital jobs. It stores extra glucose for times when your body needs it. It removes nitrogen from unnecessary amino acids and sends the nitrogen to the kidneys to be eliminated from the body. It stores fat and changes it to simpler matter. It gives blood its power to clot and makes heparin that prevents the blood from clotting inside blood vessels. It stores iron for making hemoglobin. It makes bile and sends it through small bile tubes to the gall bladder, from which it goes to the small intestine as it is needed for digestion. And finally, the liver destroys certain poisons that might get into your body.

THE LIVER

A. Makes bile.
B. Adds clotting power.
C. Makes heparin.
D. Destroys poisons.
E. Separates nitrogen from amino acids.
F. Stores fat, glucose, iron.

The Kidneys ...

The kidneys are bean shaped and about half the size of the heart. They are located just below the ribs on the right and left of the spine. They filter waste material from the blood and keep necessary material in the blood.

The thin outer part of the kidney, the cortex, has millions of tiny coiled blood vessels. Each coil is surrounded by a ball-shaped sheath into which waste passes from the blood vessels. The sheath leads the waste into many tiny collecting tubules. These are bunched together in pyramids, the points of which face a large sac, the pelvis. The pyramids make up the kidney medulla. From the pelvis the waste or urine passes into tubes, one for each kidney, called the ureters. These lead the urine down into the bladder—a muscular bag that collects the urine. When enough gathers, a ring of muscle at the lower end of the bladder relaxes and the urine passes through another tube, the urethra, out of the body.

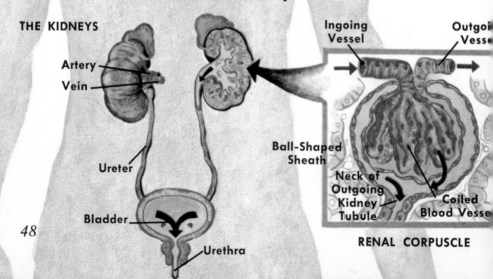

THE KIDNEYS

Artery

Vein

Ureter

Bladder

Urethra

Ingoing Vessel

Outgoing Vessel

Ball-Shaped Sheath

Neck of Outgoing Kidney Tubule

Coiled Blood Vessel

RENAL CORPUSCLE

48

6 COMMUNICATION: MESSAGES SENT AND RECEIVED

TWO SYSTEMS, the nervous and the endocrine, receive, sort, and act on messages from inside and outside your body. These two systems keep order among all the things your body does.

Two types of fibers go out from each of your nerve cells. On one side there are many short fibers, the dendrites. From the other side goes out a long fiber, the axon. All parts of your body are connected with your brain or spinal cord by such fibers.

The nerve fibers lie together in long bunches. Many bunches lie together in a sheath much like the wires in an electric cable. Such cables are called nerves. Some of these receive messages such as pain, touch, light, and sound. They send these to their cells which in turn send them to other cells or directly to the spinal cord or brain. Such nerves are sensory. The brain receives the messages, sorts them, and decides what to do about them. If action is necessary, the brain sends impulses down the motor nerves. These cause muscles to move, and so movement happens.

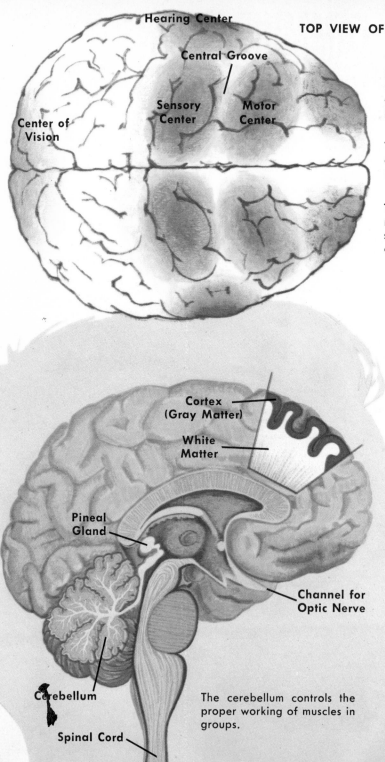

Hearing Center

Central Groove

TOP VIEW OF THE BRAIN

Sensory Center

Motor Center

Center of Vision

That part of the brain just behind the forehead is where you learn, remember, and think.

The motor center controls your muscle movements.

The sensory center receives sense messages: pain, heat, cold, and so on.

Cortex (Gray Matter)

SIDE VIEW

White Matter

Pineal Gland

Channel for Optic Nerve

Cerebellum

The cerebellum controls the proper working of muscles in groups.

Spinal Cord

The Brain...

The brain is the body's "master control board." It is an organ that fills the skull from above the eyes to just below the curve at the back of the head. It has an outer thin layer, which is grey and called the cortex. This is the seat of all your thinking and understanding. A thicker part of the brain below the cortex is white.

Of the nerves in your body, the most important are the twelve pairs of cranial nerves. These go directly to the brain, one set from each side of your body. They report what is going on in the world and make certain muscles act. These are known as the first, second, and third cranial nerves, and so on to the twelfth. By and large they serve smell, sight, hearing, taste, and speech. They control the muscles of the face, tongue and throat, and all the organs in the chest and belly. They also bring information from tiny organs, the semicircular canals, about balance. These canals are in the skull bone near the ears. There are three in number. Each canal forms a half circle —one standing upright, another lying flat, and the third at an angle. All are joined together and filled with fluid. These canals signal balance much the way a carpenter's level tells you a piece of work is or is not on the square.

Very simple messages do not always travel to the brain. Heat and pain messages are sent to the spinal cord, which sends movement impulses to the muscles. This is called a reflex action.

Sight and the Eyes

The eyeball is filled with a clear, watery liquid. It sits in and is attached to the bony socket in the skull by six muscles that also control all of its many movements. In the inner corner of the eye there is a small mound with a dot in it. Pull down your lower lid to see it. This is the opening of the tear or lacrimal duct that leads tears out of your eye and into your nose. The lacrimal gland that makes tears is just above this.

The iris, the colored part of your eye, surrounds the pupil or opening. It is covered by the cornea. Behind the pupil hangs the lens. This focuses light on the retina, the lining tissue at the back of the eye. From the retina the light message is sent to the center of vision in the brain.

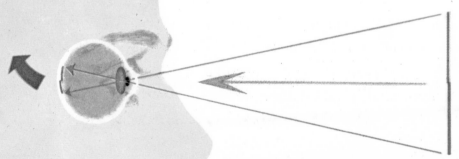

The colored part of your eye, the iris, is exactly like the diaphragm of a camera. It controls the size of the pupil or opening. Bright light narrows, dim light widens it. Covering the iris like a watch crystal is a transparent tissue, the cornea.

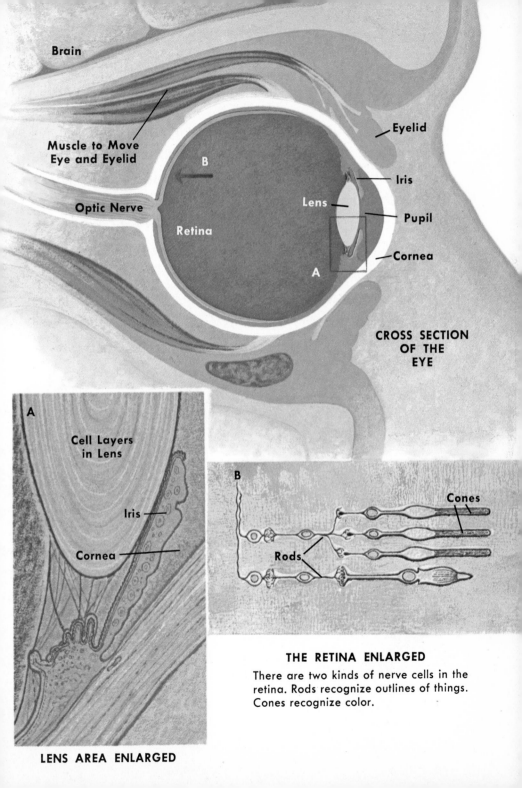

Brain

Muscle to Move Eye and Eyelid

Optic Nerve

B

Retina

A

Eyelid

Iris

Lens

Pupil

Cornea

CROSS SECTION OF THE EYE

A

Cell Layers in Lens

Iris

Cornea

LENS AREA ENLARGED

B

Cones

Rods

THE RETINA ENLARGED

There are two kinds of nerve cells in the retina. Rods recognize outlines of things. Cones recognize color.

Hearing and the Ears

The ear funnels sound into the ear canal. This causes a vibration of the ear drum, a small curtain over the inner end of the ear canal. This in turn causes three small bones, the ossicles, to vibrate. The ossicles are attached in series and cross the middle ear, a cave deeper in the skull. These in turn set up a vibration of the liquid filling the inner ear. This, shaped like a snail shell, is called the cochlea. Stretched in a spiral through it is a thin band of tissue with many fine cells and nerves which vibrate with the liquid filling it. The nerves pick up these vibrations and send them as impulses to the center of hearing in the brain. There they are translated into sound.

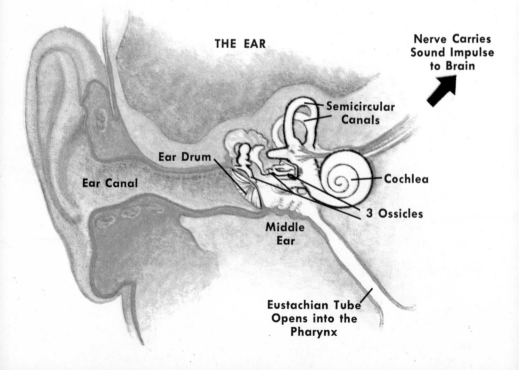

THE EAR

Nerve Carries
Sound Impulse
to Brain

Semicircular
Canals

Ear Drum

Ear Canal

Cochlea

3 Ossicles

Middle
Ear

Eustachian Tube
Opens into the
Pharynx

The Endocrine System and Hormones

The real masters of your body are chemicals called hormones. These are made by special ductless glands that send them directly into your blood stream. These glands are scattered throughout your body and together make up the endocrine system.

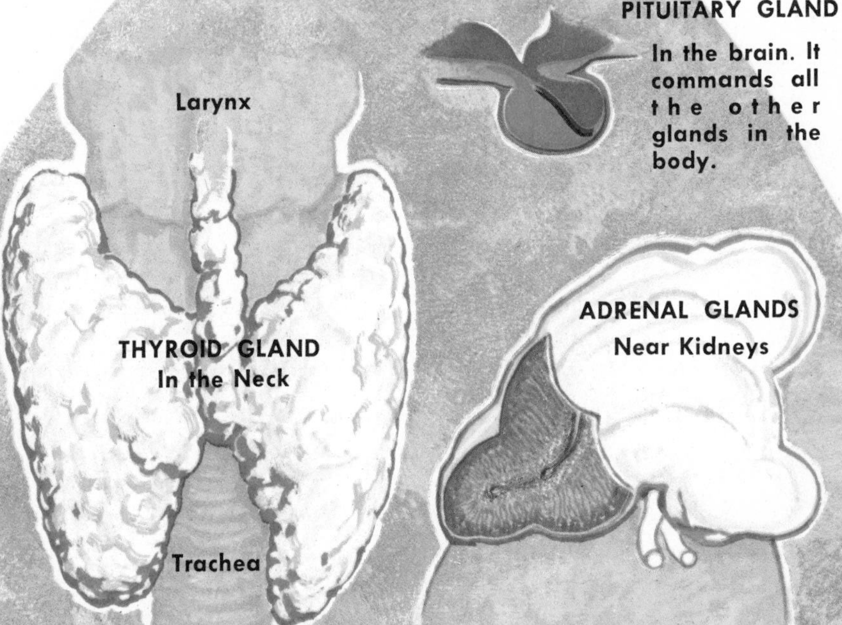

PITUITARY GLAND

In the brain. It commands all the other glands in the body.

Larynx

THYROID GLAND
In the Neck

ADRENAL GLANDS
Near Kidneys

Trachea

All of these glands and their hormones determine how strong you are; how much and how fast you will grow; how well your cells get energy from food; how fast you can act in dangerous situations; and how well and easily impulses will travel along your nerves.

7 BEFORE YOU AND AFTER

MORE REMARKABLE than cell reproduction is the type of reproduction that leads to an entirely new human being!

This starts from a combination of two entirely different cells. One is the egg or ovum made by and remaining in the female body; the other is the seed or sperm made by the male body. The ovum is many times larger than the sperm. It is made by the female body about every twenty-eight days and cannot move about by itself. The sperm, made by the male body, has a small head and a long whiplike tail that moves it about.

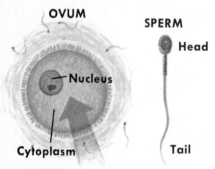

OVUM

SPERM

Head

Nucleus

Cytoplasm

Tail

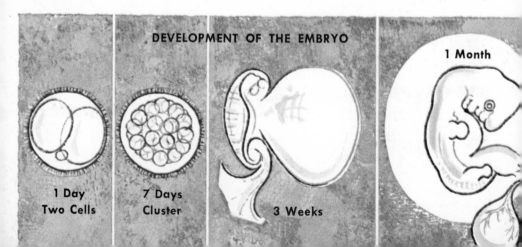

DEVELOPMENT OF THE EMBRYO

1 Day
Two Cells

7 Days
Cluster

3 Weeks

1 Month

If they are present in the female body, one of the many million sperm is bound to bump into an ovum. When this happens, the sperm goes right into the ovum. This is the beginning of a new human being.

In the ovum and head of the sperm are many long, twisted threads, the chromosomes. These cells have only half the number of chromosomes that other cells have. But when ovum and sperm join, the resulting cell has the same number of chromosomes as other cells.

At the end of one day, the new cell splits into two. The two split into four and so on until by the seventh day there is a cluster of cells that attaches itself to the mother's organ, the uterus. The cells go on multiplying. By the fourth week, the embryo, the new human being that is developing, begins to look a little like the tiny baby that will be born eight months later.

As the new human develops, the organs that will make sperm or ova are forming. Later, by joining, these will be able to make another new human being. So, you see,

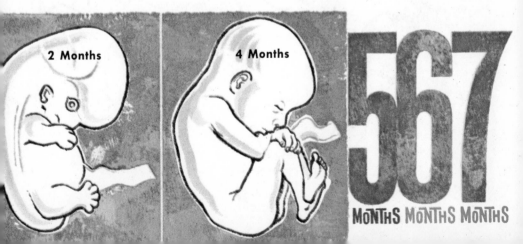

these special cells never really die!

The reproductive organs of babies are not active. They become active in the early teens when girls turn into "young ladies" and boys' voices begin to deepen and hair begins to appear on body and face. The organs develop so that when young adults marry they can have children just as their own parents had them.

In these pages you have found out much about yourself. You have learned about tissues, organs, systems, and the many other wonderful parts of your body. You have learned of the amazing way in which they work together for the good of your body as a whole. And you must agree: YOU are the most remarkable product of nature on earth!

8 MONTHS 9 MONTHS

IT'S FUN TO KNOW

. . . that a grownup's heart beats about seventy-two times a minute. The younger you are, the faster it beats. The harder you work or play, the faster it beats. Just think: the heart beats about 100,000 times a day and pumps all your blood through your entire body about two thousand times a day!

. . . that there are four types of blood: A, B, AB, and O. If the wrong types are mixed, the red cells clump together. That is why blood is tested before a transfusion.

. . . that the red cells in your blood wear out in about three weeks and are replaced.

. . . that the right half of the brain controls the left half of the body and vice versa. In right-handed people the left half of the brain is larger. In left-handed people the right half is larger. In those who can use either hand equally well, the halves of the brain are equal in size.

. . . that blood clots when it is exposed to the air. If it did not do this, even a tiny scratch would not stop bleeding.

Whitman
Learn About Books

Lots of full-color pictures and
on-the-spot photographs
Loaded with fun-to-know facts
Printed in easy-to-read type
Good sturdy bindings

11 TURN TO THE SEA *by Dr. Athelstan Spilhaus*

Learn how men of the past studied the sea, and how men of the present go down into it. Find out about the sea's strange creatures, about underwater mountains and rivers, and how one day we may farm and mine the sea.

12 CAVES AND THEIR MYSTERIES *by James McClurg*

Caves can be "live" or "dead" and can "breathe" in and out. Find out how caves form, and about soda straws, moon milk, and cave "decorations." And find out who explores caves.

13 ENGINES, PROGRESS AND POWER *by Don E. Rogers*

The first engine was a human engine, man. Learn how man found out how to make animals and water and steam work for him. Find out how gasoline engines, diesel engines, and rocket engines work.

14 YOUR BODY *by Harry Swartz, M.D.*

Learn about yourself. Find out about the cells, tissues, and organs that make up your body . . . about how bone grows and can rebuild itself when it breaks . . . and about the glands that control the workings of your body.

Whitman Learn About Books—carefully prepared with the editorial assistance of specialists in many fields.

BOOKS IN THE LEARN ABOUT SERIES

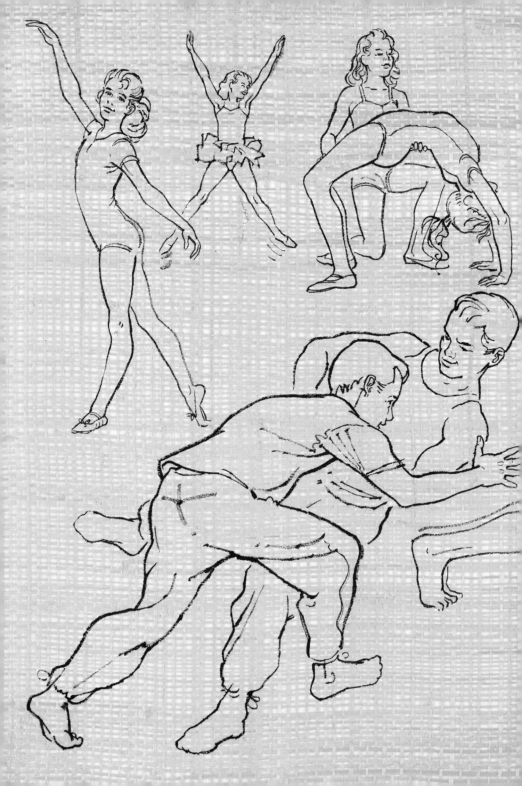